SAVING AMERICAN BEACH

The Biography of African American Environmentalist MaVynee Betsch

written by
HEIDI TYLINE KING

illustrated by Caldecott Honoree
EKUA HOLMES

putnam

G. P. Putnam's Sons

G. P. Putnam's Sons

An imprint of Penguin Random House LLC, New York

For my daughters
and Wynell Howell,
my middle school librarian
—H.T.K.

Dedicated to Yuwnus Asami and the
American Beach Museum for keeping the spirit
of American Beach alive for future generations
americanbeachmuseum.org
—E.H.

*Dreams, if they're any good,
are always a little bit crazy.*
—Ray Charles

As a girl, MaVynee Betsch loved the beach.
She loved the whoosh of its waves,
its blue sky stretching to forever,
and the creatures swimming in its tangy sea.

But MaVynee couldn't go to just any beach.

Because of her skin, silken and butter-brown,
she couldn't eat in most restaurants or visit most bathrooms.
There was even a rope in the ocean:

One side said COLORED. The other: WHITE.
Something must be done,
her great-grandfather said.

And so,
Mr. Abraham Lincoln Lewis
bought a beach.

It was an ocean paradise
where his family and other Black people
could swim, picnic, and build sandcastles.

He believed that
a beach should be open to everyone.

In no time, American Beach was hopping.

MaVynee adored her beach.
At water's edge, the sandy shore became a stage.

For each performance,
the wind whispered an endless melody
of gull cries and laughter.
It made her heart sing.

MaVynee discovered the same music in the opera.
She left her beloved beach to sing stories
around the world.

From London to Berlin, audiences sprang to their feet,
demanding an encore.
"Brava!" they cried,
beating the stage with their hands,
whipping velvet curtains into rippling waves.

But after the crowds went home
and the stage lights dimmed,
she longed for her beach.

When her mother became sick,
she packed her suitcase and
returned home to care for her.

Soon after, her mother died.

MaVynee spent her days sitting along the shore,
wrapped in a blanket of sadness.
    She sat.
        And sat.
So much had changed since her girlhood days on American Beach.

Summer houses crumbled, bleached white as fish bones.
Plastic bags littered the dunes, tangled in sea grass.

The rope dividing the ocean had disappeared.
There was no more need for a place like American Beach.

Determined to save what remained,
MaVynee became the caretaker for American Beach.
She picked up trash, planted trees,
and remembered colorful stories about its early days when
Zora Neale Hurston sunbathed on the sand
and Ray Charles juked the local joints.

She made American Beach her home.
Each morning, she bathed in the Atlantic Ocean.
Each night, she went to sleep on a chaise lounge
to a lullaby of lapping waves.

When she needed to think,
she climbed atop the beach's sixty-foot-high sand dune—
her sacred place—
one of the tallest dunes on America's East Coast.
Strong and soft, she named it *NaNa*,
a Ghanaian word for "grandmother."

Before long, builders eyed American Beach
as a perfect place for condos.

The staccato of jackhammers
replaced the whoosh of waves.
Trilling backhoes
silenced the wind's endless melody.

MaVynee was brokenhearted.
NaNa cried out to her in her dreams:
Something must be done!

She drew a line in the sand.
MaVynee was saving more than a beach.

She pinned protest buttons to her clothes,
wore seashell necklaces,
and in a burst of creative protest,
she grew her hair . . .

. . . seven feet long and knotted together,
        a thick rope of silver-gray.
She draped it over her arm or
        carried it around in a suitcase.
Some days, her hair reminded her of
        an elephant's trunk;
        on other days,
the curve of the Niger River in Africa.

It was hard to tell where
the Beach Lady stopped
and her beach began.

The madder she grew, the braver she got.
She squabbled with city commissioners,
wrote letters to lawmakers,
and marched to Tallahassee to
fuss at the governor.

Her letters went unanswered.
The Beach Lady stood in the scorching heat, alone.
No one cared what the prima donna of protest
had to say.

More than a few people questioned the Beach Lady's demands.
Others were proud of her pluck.
Years passed.

Soon, all that was left was a sliver of sand
cocooned by palmettos, hugged by live oaks.
People missed the beach.

The Beach Lady inspired others
to write their own letters and paint their own picket signs.
Together, they petitioned the president, George W. Bush,
to sign a law protecting American Beach forever.

SAVE
AMERICAN
BEACH

When the Beach Lady died,
friends and family scattered her ashes on NaNa.
Her wish came true:
to spend forever enjoying American Beach,
where a piece of paradise remains
and the melody continues.

DEFEND
MOTHER
EARTH

A NOTE *from* HEIDI

Dear Reader,

American Beach is an important site in American history. Even though importing slaves was outlawed in 1807, Spanish ships continued to smuggle human cargo into the United States. If British or U.S. ships attempted to stop them, the smugglers dumped the enslaved overboard. Their bodies washed ashore on the beach.

It was this same shore just north of Jacksonville, Florida, that would become American Beach. In the 1930s, Abraham Lincoln Lewis, founder of Florida's first insurance company and the state's first African American millionaire, bought the beach for his friends and family to enjoy, and gave it its name.

American Beach soon became a popular destination for prominent African American families. Visitors would line the streets to watch MaVynee Betsch and her family arrive with their entourage in black limousines. By day, they sunbathed; by night, they gathered at Evans' Rendezvous for performances by Ray Charles, Louis Armstrong, and Duke Ellington.

MaVynee was beautiful, intelligent, and talented. She graduated from Oberlin College and became an acclaimed opera singer on the world stage. Critics described her voice as astonishing, sovereign, and powerful.[1] But when her mother became sick, MaVynee returned home to Florida, never to sing professionally again.

Her family isn't sure why, but MaVynee sank into a profound sadness. Because she cared deeply for "all the underrepresented of the air, earth, and sea,"[2] she gave millions of dollars to save butterflies, right whales, sea turtles, African bonobos, white rhinos, Peruvian penguins, and other fragile creatures around the world.[3] Soon, she had given all her money away.[4] She moved to American Beach and spent the rest of her life trying to save it.

Because of the Beach Lady's efforts, NaNa and American Beach became part of the National Park Service and, after her death in 2005, a site on the National Register of Historic Places and Florida Black Heritage Trail. The Trust for Public Land also bought beachfront property to preserve forever.

Most operas feature an aria, a profoundly sad and emotional solo where the singer turns sorrow into something beautiful. The Beach Lady's life was an aria. In her sadness, she found renewed purpose and channeled her sadness into a powerful force for good.

XXOO
Heidi Tyline King

A NOTE *from* EKUA

It was a joy to illustrate *Saving American Beach* and to learn about an incredible artist, activist, and agent of change, MaVynee Betsch.

Many of the illustrations feature orange butterflies. Orange was MaVynee's favorite color, and she loved all the creatures of the air, especially birds, butterflies, and insects. MaVynee painted her lips and fingernails (which at one time she grew to over a foot long!) in orange as a reminder of the orange rope that was used to separate Blacks and whites at beaches during the Jim Crow era.

MaVynee's story of triumph reminds us that we are not confined to one way of making an impact on the world around us. As her grandfather used to tell her, "Understand that everything you do makes a statement, whether it's your jewelry, your clothes, or your house." In grand style, she used her voice, clothing, hair, nails, and fierce powers of persuasion to save American Beach from destruction.

At her memorial service, hundreds of orange butterflies were released to fly freely over American Beach, honoring MaVynee's tremendous and colorful spirit.

If you visit the beach today, you might feel her presence in the ever-changing sea and sky, the gulls' cries and laughter, and the melody of the whispering wind.

Ekua Holmes

1 Russ Rymer, *American Beach: A Saga of Race, Wealth, and Memory* (New York: HarperCollins, 1998).

2 Wendy Clarissa Geiger, "MaVynee Betsch," *Just Peace*, nowhereathens.com/beachladyeulogy.html (accessed January 1, 2011).

3 "MaVynee 'Beach Lady' Betsch." *The HistoryMakers: The Nation's Largest African American Video Oral History Collection*, www.thehistorymakers.org/biography/mavynee-beach-lady-betsch-39 (accessed January 31, 2020).

4 Michelle Nijhuis, "Madame Butterfly: For MaVynee Betsch, Activism Is Always a Bravura Performance," *Sierra*, September/October 2005, vault.sierraclub.org/sierra/200509/madame_butterfly.asp (accessed January 31, 2020).